T0071137

WILLIAM WALTON

TWO PIECES FOR SOLO CELLO

EDITED BY
HUGH MACDONALD

MUSIC DEPARTMENT

OXFORD
UNIVERSITY PRESS

OXFORD
UNIVERSITY PRESS

Great Clarendon Street, Oxford OX2 6DP, England
198 Madison Avenue, New York, NY 10016, USA

Oxford University Press is a department of the University of Oxford.
It furthers the University's aim of excellence in research, scholarship,
and education by publishing worldwide in

Oxford New York

Auckland Cape Town Hong Kong Karachi
Kuala Lumpur Madrid Melbourne Mexico City Nairobi
New Delhi Shanghai Taipei Toronto

With offices in

Argentina Austria Brazil Chile Czech Republic France Greece
Guatemala Hungary Italy Japan Poland Portugal Singapore
South Korea Switzerland Thailand Turkey Ukraine Vietnam

Oxford is a registered trade mark of Oxford University Press
in the UK and in certain other countries

Tema (per Variazioni) per Cello Solo © Oxford University Press 2008, 2009
Passacaglia for Violoncello Solo © Oxford University Press 1982, 2008, 2009

Database right Oxford University Press (maker)

This edition published 2009

All rights reserved. No part of this publication may be reproduced,
stored in a retrieval system, or transmitted, in any form or by any means,
without the prior permission in writing of Oxford University Press,
or as expressly permitted by law. Enquiries concerning reproduction
outside the scope of the above should be sent to the Music Copyright
Department, Oxford University Press, at the address above

Permission to perform these works in public should normally be obtained from
the Performing Right Society Ltd. (PRS), 29/33 Berners Street, London W1T 3AB,
or its affiliated Societies in each country throughout the world, unless the owner
or the occupier of the premises being used holds a licence from the Society

Permission to make a recording must be obtained in advance
from the Mechanical-Copyright Protection Society Ltd. (MCPS),
Elgar House, 41 Streatham High Road, London SW16 1ER,
or its affiliated Societies in each country throughout the world

ISBN 978–0–19–336620–6

Music origination by Enigma Music Production Services, Amersham, Bucks.
Printed in Great Britain on acid-free paper by
Caligraving Ltd., Thetford, Norfolk

Tema (per Variazioni) per Cello Solo
(from Music for a Prince)

WILLIAM WALTON

Copyright by Oxford University Press 2008, 2009.
Printed in Great Britain

OXFORD UNIVERSITY PRESS, MUSIC DEPARTMENT, GREAT CLARENDON STREET, OXFORD OX2 6DP
The Moral Rights of the Composer have been asserted. Photocopying this copyright material is ILLEGAL.

for Mstislav Rostropovich

Passacaglia
for Violoncello Solo

Edited by Mstislav Rostropovich

WILLIAM WALTON

Copyright 1982 by Oxford University Press, London. New edition © 2008, 2009.

6